CW00498241

XANAKU

Righteous haikus and bodacious layout by
Jake Spencer

With radical illustrations by
Eric Dusseault

And gnarly editing by
Danielle S. Bouchard

WHIP IT
DEVO -- 1980

Whip it into shape.
Brushing only goes so far.
You need Aqua Net.

FUNKYTOWN
LIPPS, INC. -- 1980

Gotta make a move.
Funkytown evicted me.
There was a scandal...

ALL OUT OF LOVE
AIR SUPPLY -- 1980

I'm all out of love.
Please deposit fifty cents
For five more minutes.

BACK IN BLACK
AC/DC -- 1980

I'm back in black, cause
It didn't sound as edgy
Being back in mauve.

CALL ME
BLONDIE -- 1980

Call me! Any time!
Or you could even fax me.
I'll make love to that.

02

MAGIC
OLIVIA NEWTON-JOHN -- 1980

You have to believe,
Or else magic doesn't work,
And we are nothing.

GIVE ME THE NIGHT
GEORGE BENSON -- 1980

Music in the air
Is keeping me from sleeping.
Just give me the night.

BIGGEST PART OF ME
AMBROSIA -- 1980

I fear surgery!
This tumor has become the
Biggest part of me.

FAME
IRENE CARA -- 1980

Remember my name.
I'm gonna live forever,
As I haunt your house.

ONCE IN A LIFETIME
TALKING HEADS -- 1980

You may find yourself
Behind the wheel of a
Van while tripping balls.

SAILING
CHRISTOPHER CROSS -- 1980

Sailing takes me there -
Away to where I'm always
White and privileged.

LONDON CALLING
THE CLASH -- 1980

Does anyone have
The London foggiest clue
What the hell he said?

TURNING JAPANESE
THE VAPORS -- 1980

You and that ramen...
Are you turning Japanese?
I wouldn't think so.

TAKE IT ON THE RUN
REO SPEEDWAGON -- 1981

Take it on the run -
That's why all the restaurants
Have a drive-thru now.

BRASS IN POCKET
THE PRETENDERS -- 1980

I'll make him notice.
Gonna use most body parts,
Except for my brain.

06

UNDER PRESSURE
QUEEN & DAVID BOWIE -- 1981

Sometimes I'm contrite
When I'm watching some good friends
Screaming "Let me out!"

CELEBRATION
KOOL & THE GANG -- 1981

Celebrate good times.
Post passive-aggressive tweets
About the bad times.

WHO CAN IT BE NOW
MEN AT WORK -- 1981

Damn solicitors...
Despite barbed wire and dogs,
Who can it be now?

ANGEL OF THE MORNING
JUICE NEWTON -- 1981

Yeah, call me "Angel",
Unlike "Mr. Hungover",
And "Dead to the World".

IN THE AIR TONIGHT
PHIL COLLINS -- 1981

I feel it coming.
You'll know, in the air tonight,
I had burritos.

WHILE YOU SEE A CHANCE
STEVE WINWOOD -- 1981

Tired of gridlock?
While you see a chance, take it.
(Just pass on the left).

BETTE DAVIS EYES
KIM CARNES -- 1981

Bette Davis eyes
Are sadly lost behind her
Alfred Hitchcock jowls.

DON'T YOU WANT ME
HUMAN LEAGUE -- 1981

Tell me you want me.
Baby, you know I'm fragile.
Please validate me.

THEME FROM GREATEST AMERICAN HERO
JOEY SCARBURY -- 1981

Believe it or not,
As I plummet to my death,
I'm walking on air.

DON'T STOP BELIEVING
JOURNEY -- 1981

How can I believe
In a midnight train that goes
To just some small town?

10

Teen Witch

EVERY LITTLE THING SHE DOES IS MAGIC
THE POLICE - 1981

The big things are lame,
However, the little things
Are quite magical.

KEEP ON LOVING YOU
REO SPEEDWAGON -- 1981

Restraining orders
Mean I must try harder to
Keep on loving you.

DA DA DA
TRIO -- 1981

I found this button
On my Casio keyboard;
Instant chart-topper.

MORNING TRAIN
SHEENA EASTON -- 1981

Nine to five, I wait.
My baby has a job/life.
Guess I'm a waiter.

LET MY LOVE OPEN THE DOOR
PETE TOWNSEND -- 1981

The door to your heart
Is also called "aorta".
Hope you don't bleed out.

HUNGRY HEART
BRUCE SPRINGSTEEN -- 1981

When you're all alone,
Porn, tissues, and Vaseline
Feed a hungry heart.

14

UP WHERE WE BELONG
JOE COCKER & JENNIFER WARNES -- 1982

Eagles keep flying
Into our high, mountain love.
Sure we belong here?

PASS THE DUTCHIE
MUSICAL YOUTH -- 1982

Come on, Jamaica...
Don't you strive to be more than
Pot ambassadors?

ABRACADABRA
STEVE MILLER BAND — 1982

Abracadabra.
I shan't describe my wish to
Violate your rights.

867-5309 (JENNY)
TOMMY TUTONE — 1982

I saw your number,
But then I gasped, because it
Was right next to mine.

EYE OF THE TIGER
SURVIVOR — 1982

I'm getting stronger.
Thanks, protein powder laced with
Eye of the tiger.

YOU CAN'T HURRY LOVE
PHIL COLLINS -- 1982

First, there's the waiting.
Then, there's giving and taking.
After that, it's love.

CENTERFOLD
J GEILS BAND -- 1982

My homeroom angel
Is a centerfold, which means
Heaven is porno.

BEAT IT
MICHAEL JACKSON -- 1982

No one likes defeat.
It's not about right or wrong,
You just didn't win.

SHOULD I STAY OR SHOULD I GO
THE CLASH -- 1982

I'm still wondering
Why you even showed up here
In the first place, bro.

HARDEN MY HEART
QUARTERFLASH -- 1982

I'll harden my heart
After I smash your headlights
And chat with your wife.

18

EBONY & IVORY
PAUL MCCARTNEY & STEVIE WONDER -- 1982

My piano keys?
Ivory or ebony?
It says "Yamaha"...

WHITE WEDDING
BILLY IDOL -- 1982

I dig white weddings,
But what drives me wild is
A black honeymoon.

BACK ON THE CHAIN GANG
THE PRETENDERS -- 1982

I was hit by trash.
Thanks, traffic. It's great to be
Back on the chain gang...

TAINTED LOVE
SOFT CELL -- 1982

The worst kind of love.
It taint the front or the back,
If you catch my drift.

PHYSICAL
OLIVIA NEWTON-JOHN -- 1982

As for animals,
If you hear their bodies talk,
That's indigestion.

LITTLE RED CORVETTE
PRINCE -- 1982

Little red Corvette,
How can something so pretty
Make so much exhaust?

OUR HOUSE
MADNESS -- 1982

That's a huge hazard...
Isn't that our house in the
Middle of the street?!

MANEATER
HALL & OATES -- 1982

Yes, she was just here.
You should have been here last night;
Saw her eat a man!

SHE BLINDED ME WITH SCIENCE
THOMAS DOLBY -- 1982

Then she deafened me
With Western History, and
Bludgeoned me with Math.

RIO
DURAN DURAN -- 1982

She danced in the sand,
Until she saw used condoms
And cigarette butts.

22

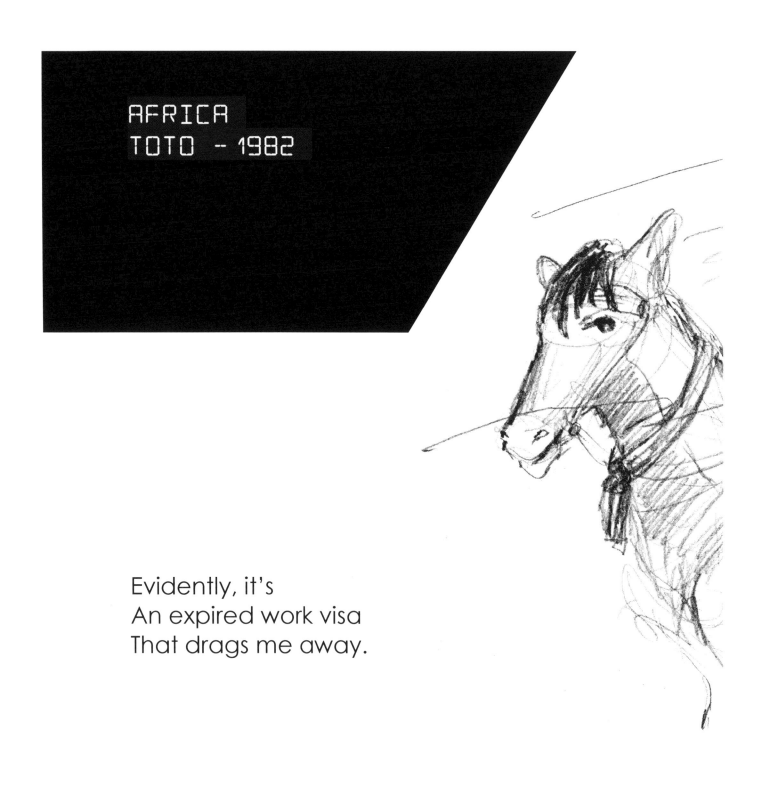

AFRICA
TOTO -- 1982

Evidently, it's
An expired work visa
That drags me away.

Sahara

SOMEBODY'S BABY
JACKSON BROWNE -- 1982

She's got to be, right?
Save for immaculate birth,
She must have parents.

HEY MICKEY
TONI BASIL -- 1983

Ouch! Dammit, my head!
I think my mind has been blown.
Why are you so fine?!

HURTS SO GOOD
JOHN MELLENCAMP -- 1982

"Sometimes love don't feel
Like it should. It hurts so good."
-That's what rapists say.

WAITING FOR A GIRL LIKE YOU
FOREIGNER -- 1982

Do you know how long
I've been waiting for you, girl?
Oh... It's a gay bar?

THRILLER
MICHAEL JACKSON -- 1982

After thriller night,
We had a moaning morning
And then brains for brunch.

26

TOTAL ECLIPSE OF THE HEART
BONNIE TYLER -- 1983

During the eclipse,
It was dark and I was lost.
At least my heart was...

OWNER OF A LONELY HEART
YES -- 1983

My heart is lonely,
But at least I found a friend
For my lonely hand.

SUDDENLY LAST SUMMER
THE MOTELS — 1983

We banged in your car.
And, suddenly, this summer,
Here is your daughter.

ALL NIGHT LONG
LIONEL RICHIE — 1983

We're gonna party.
Yes, there'll be alcohol. No,
It's not a bender.

ELECTRIC AVENUE
EDDY GRANT — 1983

You just rolled a nine.
I also own Water Works.
That's ninety dollars.

LOVE IS A BATTLEFIELD
PAT BENATAR -- 1983

Heartache to heartache
We stand, then kill each other,
Both of us knowing...

MR. ROBOTO
STYX - 1983

"Mr. Roboto"
Would be great for marketing.
Someone get on this.

MANIAC
MICHAEL SEMBELLO - 1983

Whoa! Is she ok?
I've never seen her dancing
So manic like that.

ONE THING LEADS TO ANOTHER
THE FIXX -- 1983

You know something, right…
One thing leads to another,
And now I'm pregnant.

BURNING DOWN THE HOUSE
TALKING HEADS -- 1983

This is bang music
And a sex euphemism:
Burning down the house.

THAT'S WHY THEY CALL IT THE BLUES
ELTON JOHN -- 1983

I have two choices:
I could spend time with you, or,
Then again, these hands...

IN A BIG COUNTRY
BIG COUNTRY -- 1983

Like a lover's voice
Across the mountainside is
Hillbilly phone sex.

HUNGRY LIKE THE WOLF
DURAN DURAN -- 1983

You smell like you sound.
That is to say you smell like
A wolf with big hair.

SEND ME AN ANGEL
REAL LIFE -- 1983

Ground shipping is fine.
I'm gonna need that devil
Overnighted, please.

TRUE
SPANDAU BALLET -- 1983

I know this much is...
Well, when you get to my age,
Who knows what is true?

EYES WITHOUT A FACE
BILLY IDOL -- 1983

They rest in a jar,
Swimming in formaldehyde
Atop your neck stump.

SEXUAL HEALING
MARVIN GAYE -- 1983

It's an STD.
So, when you get that feeling,
You should use ointment.

BLISTER IN THE SUN
VIOLENT FEMMES -- 1983

I'd much rather be
A blister in the sun than
A sore in the rain.

GIRLS JUST WANT TO HAVE FUN
CYNDI LAUPER -- 1983

On the internet,
Girls just want to have fun, and
Boys just want to watch.

LAND DOWN UNDER
MEN AT WORK -- 1983

Yes, I can hear them.
How men and women thunder,
I may never know.

34

1999
PRINCE - 1983

I'm gonna party
With take-out and porn like it's
1999.

Weird Science

SWEET DREAMS
EURYTHMICS -- 1983

I traveled and searched
Half of the world and three seas,
And then I found it.

I'M STILL STANDING
ELTON JOHN -- 1983

Three words for standing
Better than I ever did:
Dual hip replacement.

EVERY BREATH YOU TAKE
THE POLICE -- 1983

I know you watch me,
So I learned to stop breathing
And making moves, too.

ISLANDS IN THE STREAM
DOLLY PARTON & KENNY ROGERS -- 1983

Islands in the stream,
Luring ships to their demise,
That is what we are.

COME ON EILEEN
DEXY'S MIDNIGHT RUNNERS -- 1983

Without a comma,
You did something so nasty
To that poor Eileen.

38

WAKE ME UP BEFORE YOU GO-GO
WHAM -- 1984

Your tenacity
Is stronger than a yo-yo.
Keep hanging in there!

YOU SPIN ME AROUND
DEAD OR ALIVE -- 1984

You spin me around.
How can you say it's my fault
I puked on your feet?

NEVERENDING STORY
LIMAHL -- 1984

Despite the title,
The book never ends, but the
Song is four minutes.

SMOOTH OPERATOR
SADE -- 1984

She'll connect your call
After complimenting you
Through sexy whispers.

KARMA CHAMELEON
CULTURE CLUB -- 1984

I really left home
Wearing red, gold, and green clothes.
I wasn't dreaming!

SUNGLASSES AT NIGHT
COREY HART -- 1984

I wear sunglasses
At all times, even at night,
Thanks to glaucoma.

INTO THE GROOVE
MADONNA -- 1984

Is "groove" a rhyme word?
Sexual innuendo?
Get into your what?

SOMEBODY'S WATCHING ME
ROCKWELL -- 1984

Somebody's watching.
YouTube keeps a count for me.
I'm going viral!

ROCK YOU LIKE A HURRICANE
THE SCORPIONS -- 1984

Or, if you prefer,
I'll roll you like a mudslide.
Sexy options, right?

I WANT TO BREAK FREE
QUEEN -- 1984

I have to punch out
For fifteen minutes outside?
I want to break free.

42

I WANT TO KNOW WHAT LOVE IS
FOREIGNER -- 1984

Can you show me, please?
Love is undefined in my
User manual.

ONE NIGHT IN BANGKOK
MURRAY HEAD -- 1984

One night in Bangkok
Away from western morals
Should take the edge off.

TALKING IN YOUR SLEEP
THE ROMANTICS -- 1984

I hear your secrets.
Guess I'll wait to see you on
"Catch a Predator".

SUMMER OF '69
BRYAN ADAMS -- 1984

Forget forever.
I'm not doing kinky sex
On my momma's porch.

CRUEL SUMMER
BANANARAMA -- 1984

It's a cruel summer,
But, thanks to global warming,
It's January.

LET THE MUSIC PLAY
SHANNON -- 1984

Let the music play.
He'll come back to you, but then,
So will other men.

I MISS YOU
KLYMAXX -- 1984

I can't deny it.
Whenever the seat is up,
That's when I miss you.

SELF-CONTROL
LAURA BRANIGAN -- 1984

Take my self-control.
(That means it wasn't really
Mine in the first place.)

THE WARRIOR
SCANDAL FEAT. PATTY SMYTH -- 1984

I got arrested.
Heartache called the cops on me
Shooting at the walls.

CARIBBEAN QUEEN
BILLY OCEAN -- 1984

In this dream we share,
Do you think our love must run
Because it can't swim?

46

Baby Boom

HOW SOON IS NOW
THE SMITHS -- 1984

I am human and
I need to be fed and burped.
Oh, and also loved.

TIME AFTER TIME
CYNDI LAUPER -- 1984

Yes, I'm here for you.
But how come you keep falling
And getting so lost?

IT'S MY LIFE
TALK TALK -- 1984

Funny how I find
Myself so in love with you,
Since you're dead and all...

JUMP
POINTER SISTERS -- 1984

Just jump for my love,
Somersault for friendship, or
Bend over for sex.

THEME FROM GHOSTBUSTERS
RAY PARKER JR -- 1984

Invisible man:
He's something strange in my bed.
I call that fun, though.

HOLD ME NOW
THOMPSON TWINS -- 1984

Hold me in your arms.
I have a fetish for the
Fetal position.

50

WHAT'S LOVE GOT TO DO WITH IT
TINA TURNER -- 1984

It's a hookup site.
What's love got to do with it?
I don't need your name.

OUT OF TOUCH
HALL & OATES -- 1984

We're on Ecstasy.
With you, I'm out of my head
When E *is* around.

DANCING WITH TEARS IN MY EYES
                ULTRAVOX -- 1984

What did you expect?
You went to the prom with a
Dress made of onions.

DRIVE
THE CARS -- 1984

Who's gonna drive you?
You know how the saying goes:
It's gas, grass, or ass.

RUNNING UP THAT HILL
        KATE BUSH -- 1985

If I only could
Make a deal with god, then
I wouldn't be here.

RASPBERRY BERET
PRINCE -- 1985

Today, kids would guess
It's a sex euphemism
Or a smartphone app.

VOICES CARRY
TIL TUESDAY -- 1985

Shush! Keep it down now.
I'm listening to music.
Oh, the irony.

SUSSUDIO
PHIL COLLINS -- 1985

Oh, just say the word...
At least try sounding it out...
Soo-soo-soo-dee-oh.

EVERYBODY WANTS TO RULE THE WORLD
TEARS FOR FEARS -- 1985

Nah. I'm pretty sure
There are lots of folks out there
Happy being sheep.

WE BUILT THIS CITY
STARSHIP -- 1985

It was rock and roll,
Until yuppies moved in with
Noise ordinances.

54

WALKING ON SUNSHINE
KATRINA AND THE WAVES -- 1985

Walking on sunshine
Is starting to feel good.
These are great mushrooms!

BOYS OF SUMMER
DON HENLEY -- 1985

Oh so many boys,
After so little summer.
I'll still love you, though.

THERE MUST BE AN ANGEL
EURYTHMICS -- 1985

It's a heart attack.
"Suddenly my heart goes boom"?
Screw this angel talk.

TAKE ON ME
A--HA -- 1985

Dah dah dah dah dah,
Dah dah, dah dadadada,
Dah dah dah dah dah.

SHOUT
TEARS FOR FEARS -- 1985

Shout. Let it all out.
Wait, don't get carried away!
You vomited blood.

EVERY TIME YOU GO AWAY
PAUL YOUNG -- 1985

Please don't go away.
There are few pieces of me,
And I'm running out.

MATERIAL GIRL
MADONNA -- 1985

By "material",
I'm talking fishnets, pleather,
And cones on my boobs.

HEAVEN
BRYAN ADAMS -- 1985

My arm fell asleep;
You've been lying here too long.
That's all that you want?

ST ELMO'S FIRE (MAN IN MOTION)
JOHN PARR -- 1985

I need some wheels
In order to have motion.
See, my car's on blocks.

LAST CHRISTMAS
WHAM -- 1985

I gave you my heart,
And on the very next day
I was cremated.

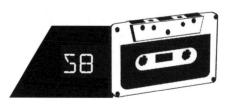

58

Summer School

MIAMI VICE THEME
JAN HAMMER — 1985

Miami Vice theme:
For when "business casual"
Means "sleeveless pastel".

YOU CAN CALL ME AL
PAUL SIMON -- 1986

You can call me Al;
Don't call me late for dinner.
(Yeah, a lame dad joke).

FASCINATED
COMPANY B -- 1986

I'm fascinated.
The wigs, outfits, and makeup
Are really something...

SLEDGEHAMMER
PETER GABRIEL -- 1986

...Or are you more of
The kind of girl who likes a
Piledriver? (Wink)

DON'T YOU (FORGET ABOUT ME)
SIMPLE MINDS -- 1985

As you walk on by,
Call my name or hold a sign,
Like at the airport.

SAY YOU, SAY ME
LIONEL RICHIE -- 1986

Say it together.
That's just the way it should be:
Something more like "myoo".

62

FIGHT FOR YOUR RIGHT TO PARTY
BEASTIE BOYS -- 1986

Is it ironic,
Though, that you gotta party
For your right to fight?

ADDICTED TO LOVE
ROBERT PALMER -- 1986

Immune to what stuff?
Might as well face addiction.
You'll need a sponsor.

TAKE MY BREATH AWAY
BERLIN -- 1986

It was slow motion
As you literally knocked
The wind out of me.

BROKEN WINGS
MR MISTER -- 1986

Like riding a bike -
Even with those broken wings
You retain flying.

TOUCH ME
SAMANTHA FOX -- 1986

Oh, wait a minute...
I wanna feel your body,
So I should touch you.

GREATEST LOVE OF ALL
WHITNEY HOUSTON -- 1986

I'm so sunburned, but
You know where I never walked?
Anyone's shadow.

YOUR LOVE
THE OUTFIELD -- 1986

So, about your love...
If I do lose it tonight,
Check the couch cushions.

DON'T DREAM IT'S OVER
CROWDED HOUSE -- 1986

Don't dream it's over.
I still have many bizarre
Metaphors for you.

THE FUTURE'S SO BRIGHT,
I GOTTA WEAR SHADES
TIMBUK3 – 1986

I gotta wear shades.
These eyes share the secret of
My very dark past.

GLORY OF LOVE
PETER CETERA – 1986

Why am I fighting
For the honor you simply
Insist on losing?

66

WHEN I THINK OF YOU
JANET JACKSON -- 1986

I'm thinking of you.
Nothing else matters. Ooh, ahh…
I have lost myself.

WEST END GIRLS
PET SHOP BOYS -- 1986

The town and refrain
Have plenty of boys and girls,
But no predicates.

HUMAN
HUMAN LEAGUE -- 1986

I'm only human.
These organs sell for a mint.
I'm worth way more dead.

GIRLFRIEND
PEBBLES -- 1987

He's in prison now.
You're the best he ever had.
Now he's someone's bitch.

HOW WILL I KNOW
WHITNEY HOUSTON - 1986

The Magic 8-Ball
Knows if he really loves you.
Step right up, my dear.

NOTHING'S GONNA STOP US NOW
STARSHIP -- 1987

Hi, is this Venus?
Can you please send more lovers?
This world just ran out.

CHINA IN YOUR HAND
T'PAU -- 1987

Dreams are delicate.
Better China in your hand
Than Guam in your butt.

BEDS ARE BURNING
MIDNIGHT OIL -- 1987

The beds are burning,
But I can sleep thanks to these
Kevlar pajamas.

I STILL HAVEN'T FOUND
WHAT I'M LOOKING FOR
U2 - 1987

...And I may never.
Losing a contact lens sucks.
Drugs are not helping.

I NEED YOU TONIGHT
INXS - 1987

I need you tonight.
We're talking life or death here.
You are life support.

70

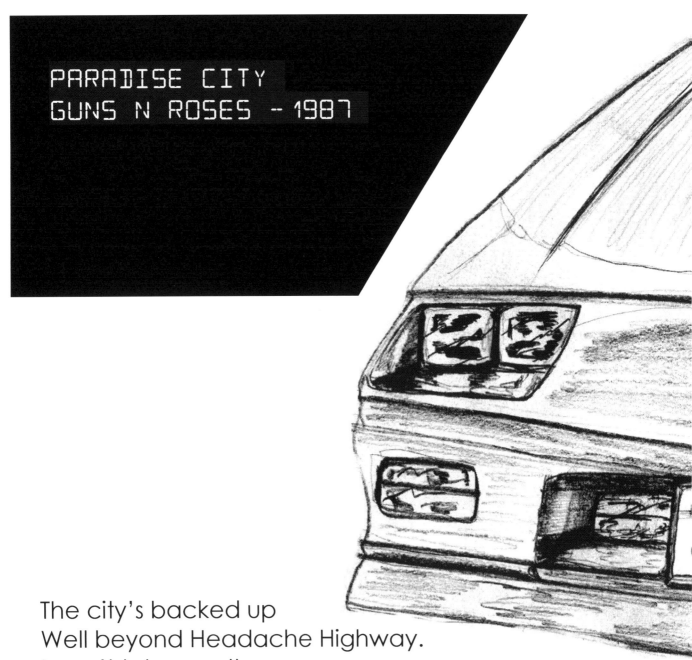

PARADISE CITY
GUNS N ROSES - 1987

The city's backed up
Well beyond Headache Highway.
I can't take you there.

Adventures in Babysitting

HEAVEN IS A PLACE ON EARTH
BELINDA CARLISLE -- 1987

I know it comes first,
But how would I know its worth?
Is it real estate?

MONY MONY
BILLY IDOL -- 1987

Yeah! Ride the pony!
Macaroni! Telephone
Me! Eat Baloney!

LIVIN' ON A PRAYER
BON JOVI -- 1987

We've gone like half way,
And now, in doubt, you decide
To take my damn hand.

NEVER GONNA GIVE YOU UP
RICK ASTLEY -- 1987

Sorry, I can't claim
I'll never spend your money,
Or leave the seat up.

WITH OR WITHOUT YOU
U2 -- 1987

Yes, it's about you.
Although, if I kill myself,
It's all about me.

74

I THINK WE'RE ALONE NOW
TIFFANY -- 1987

Just what would who say?
There ain't anyone around.
Let's take a selfie.

THE ONE I LOVE
REM -- 1987

This one goes out to
A pepperoni pizza.
It's the one I love.

WALK LIKE AN EGYPTIAN
THE BANGLES -- 1987

Egyptians don't walk
With bent hands jabbing forward.
That's how racists walk.

HERE I GO AGAIN
WHITESNAKE -- 1987

I go on my own.
I was born to walk alone,
And talk to myself.

THE LADY IN RED
CHRIS DE BURGH -- 1987

She calls it dancing.
We're rubbing butts together,
She says: "Cheek to cheek".

DUDE LOOKS LIKE A LADY
AEROSMITH -- 1987

Dude's self-confident
Rocking whatever he wants,
Without your input.

LET ME BE THE ONE
EXPOSE -- 1987

Yes, I realize
This is your seventh marriage.
Let me be "the one".

ALWAYS
ATLANTIC STARR -- 1987

If you are the sun
And you've chased the rain away,
How will our love grow?

WISHING WELL
TERENCE TRENT D'ARBY -- 1987

I don't understand.
Do you wish for my love, or
An actual well?

FAITH
GEORGE MICHAEL -- 1987

Yes, it would be nice.
I can't touch, though, due to a
Restraining order.

78

HEAD TO TOE
LISA LISA & CULT JAM -- 1987

I think I love you
From head to toe, however,
Some parts are better.

HANDS TO HEAVEN
BREATHE -- 1988

I love your caress
And the way you're holding me,
But damn, do you snore!

SHATTERED DREAMS
JOHNNY HATES JAZZ – 1987

You have given me
Nothing but my shattered dreams
And gonorrhea.

ALONE
HEART – 1987

No. Never, really.
I cared about not one thing.
Until I met you.

MAN IN THE MIRROR
MICHAEL JACKSON – 1988

Man in the mirror
Tries, but he cannot reach, the
Kids in the closet.

I'LL BE THERE FOR YOU
BON JOVI -- 1988

I'll be there for you,
But this is a text message.
Don't know where "there" is.

KOKOMO
BEACH BOYS -- 1988

No one knows this place.
Sure, we've all heard about it.
Find it on this map...

TOGETHER FOREVER
RICK ASTLEY -- 1988

And never to part?
Is this a relationship
Or a life sentence?

GOT MY MIND SET ON YOU
GEORGE HARRISON -- 1988

I've got my mind set.
You're with an obstinate man.
I mean that with love.

POUR SOME SUGAR ON ME
DEF LEPPARD - 1988

Pour sugar on me.
It helps me forget about
My diabetes.

82

Burglar

STRAIGHT OUTTA COMPTON
NWA -- 1988

Straight outta Compton,
With layovers in Newark
And Cincinnati.

TELL IT TO MY HEART
TAYLOR DAYNE -- 1988

Is this really love
Or just a game? If it is,
Let's play sex instead.

THE FLAME
CHEAP TRICK -- 1988

After the rain, sure.
But why flame after fire?
Isn't that like "Duh"?

SO EMOTIONAL
WHITNEY HOUSTON -- 1988

I think about you;
I get called emotional.
You shout at TV.

GET OUTTA MY DREAMS, GET INTO MY CAR
BILLY OCEAN -- 1988

Get into your car?
I'm sure a total stranger
Simply wants to chat.

HOLD ON TO THE NIGHTS
RICHARD MARX -- 1988

Hold on to the nights,
Juggle all of the weekends,
And write off the days.

86

HANGIN' TOUGH
NEW KIDS ON THE BLOCK -- 1988

To combat swelling,
Hangin' became shrinkin' from
The ice on my crotch.

SHAKE YOUR LOVE
DEBBIE GIBSON -- 1988

Remember to shake
And aim away from your face.
Love is aerosol.

FATHER FIGURE
GEORGE MICHAEL -- 1988

This song ought to win
The NAMBLA award for sure.
Be my daddy, George.

THE LOOK
ROXETTE -- 1989

That brown-eyed girl there
Is staring...oh...she turned blue.
Help her; she's choking!

THING CALLED LOVE
BONNIE RAITT -- 1989

Are you ready for
Cohabitation and kids:
It's a thing called love?

PERSONAL JESUS
DEPECHE MODE -- 1989

Reach out and touch faith.
(Insert joke here about the
Church's sex scandal).

TOY SOLDIERS
MARTIKA -- 1989

When I was a kid,
I always heard "Left, right, left,
Now turn and cough." Heh.

BUFFALO STANCE
NENEH CHERRY -- 1989

Buffalo stance is
The way we hang, instead of
Cheese and/or cool ranch.

SHE DRIVES ME CRAZY
FINE YOUNG CANNIBALS -- 1989

She drives me crazy.
Good thing chicks dig guys who are
Certifiable.

POISON
ALICE COOPER -- 1989

I want to kiss you,
But your lips are... compromised.
That scab is suspect.

90

IF I COULD TURN BACK TIME
CHER -- 1989

I could reach the stars,
But I would combust, so I
Can't give them to you.

STRAIGHT UP
PAULA ABDUL -- 1989

Straight up, now tell me,
Is it gonna be the you
In your profile?

LIKE A PRAYER
MADONNA -- 1989

Not quite a sermon,
And nowhere near the "oomph" of
Evangelical.

JUST A FRIEND
BIZ MARKIE -- 1989

You say he's a friend,
But it smells like sex in here.
Friend with benefits?

RIGHT HERE WAITING
RICHARD MARX -- 1989

Wherever you go,
Whatever you do, I'll wait.
#ForeverAlone

LISTEN TO YOUR HEART
ROXETTE -- 1989

Please tell your doctor
About shortness of breath, sweats,
Or pain in your arm.

REAL LOVE
JODY WATLEY -- 1989

I'm looking for it.
Just no vampires, werewolves,
Or shades of grey rape.

HEAD LIKE A HOLE
NINE INCH NAILS -- 1989

The booze falls down it,
Through your belly like a drum,
To your hollow leg.

SOWING THE SEEDS OF LOVE
TEARS FOR FEARS -- 1989

At this rate I'll be
Raking the leaves of divorce
Come late September.

BEEN AROUND THE WORLD
LISA STANSFIELD -- 1989

I am the mother
Of Carmen San Diego.
Can't find my baby.

94

ROAM
THE B-52'S - 1989

"Take it hip to hip.
Rocket through the wilderness",
Means "Stick it in me".

Stranger Than Paradise

THE JUKEBOX

THE JUKEBOX

THE JUKEBOX

"Personally curated for you (unapologetically heavy on the new wave sound) and for the best 80's experience you can imagine." -Jake

Psychedelic Furs - The Ghost in You (1984)

The Waterboys - The Pan Within (1985)

Real Life - Send Me an Angel (1983)

Tears for Fears - Year of the Knife (1989)

The Stabilizers - One Simple Thing (1986)

The Outfield - Since You've Been Gone (1987)

Philip Jap - Brain Dance (1983)

Level 42 - Something About You (1985)

Belinda Carlisle - Fool for Love (1987)

Benjamin Orr - In Circles (1986)

Thomas Dolby - Europa and the Pirate Twins (1981)

Berlin - Now It's My Turn (1984)

Peter Godwin - Images of Heaven (1982)

Missing Persons - Color in Your Life (1986)

Midge Ure - If I Was (1985)

Industry - State of the Nation (1983)

Big Bam Boo - If You Could See Me Now (1989)

Melissa Manchester - You Should Hear How She Talks about You (1982)

Dare - The Raindance (1988)

Virginia Wolf - For All We Know (1986)

Alphaville - Forever Young (1984)

Printed in Great
Britain
by Amazon